SOURCES OF FORCES
SCIENCE FUN WITH FORCE FIELDS

VICKI COBB
ILLUSTRATED BY STEVE HAEFELE

THE MILLBROOK PRESS
BROOKFIELD, CONNECTICUT

Published by The Millbrook Press, Inc.
2 Old New Milford Road
Brookfield, CT 06804
www.millbrookpress.com

Library of Congress Cataloging-in-Publication Data
Cobb, Vicki.
Sources of forces : science fun with force fields / by Vicki Cobb ; illustrated by Steve Haefele.
p. cm.
Summary: Text and simple experiments introduce electrical, magnetic, and gravitational force fields.
ISBN 0-7613-1574-8 (lib. bdg.)
1. Magnetism—Experiments—Juvenile literature. 2. Electricity—Experiments—Juvenile literature.
[1. Electricity—Experiments. 2. Magnetism—Experiments. 3. Experiments.] I. Haefele, Steve, ill. II. Title
QC753.7. C63 2002
538'.078—dc21   2001042804

Visit Vicki Cobb at www.vickicobb.com

1  POWERS OF ATTRACTION

Imagine that you had a rock with super powers. It could make things move without touching them. Sounds impossible? But it's true.

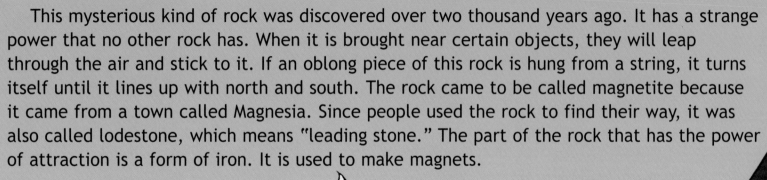

This mysterious kind of rock was discovered over two thousand years ago. It has a strange power that no other rock has. When it is brought near certain objects, they will leap through the air and stick to it. If an oblong piece of this rock is hung from a string, it turns itself until it lines up with north and south. The rock came to be called magnetite because it came from a town called Magnesia. Since people used the rock to find their way, it was also called lodestone, which means "leading stone." The part of the rock that has the power of attraction is a form of iron. It is used to make magnets.

5

An Ancient Greek named Thales discovered another substance that had mysterious powers of attraction. Thales had been given some beautiful yellow beads. The beads were made from pine sap that had become as hard as stone. When Thales polished a bead with a cloth, it attracted bits of thread from his polishing cloth.

The bead also attracted small bits of straw. If Thales ran his hand over the bead, it lost its power of attraction. But the power came back when he rubbed the bead again. The Greeks called this material "elecktros." We call it amber. Amber is used today in jewelry. Can you guess what word comes from elecktros?

ELECTRICITY, DUH!

How close does an object have to be to a magnet or rubbed amber before it jumps through the air and sticks to it?

THIS IS THE KIND OF QUESTION SCIENTISTS ASK. NO ONE HAS TO TELL YOU THE ANSWER. YOU CAN EXPERIMENT AND FIND OUT FOR YOURSELF.

The area around a magnet or a piece of rubbed amber that has the power of attraction is called a "field of force." Magnets and amber do not attract anything outside their force fields.

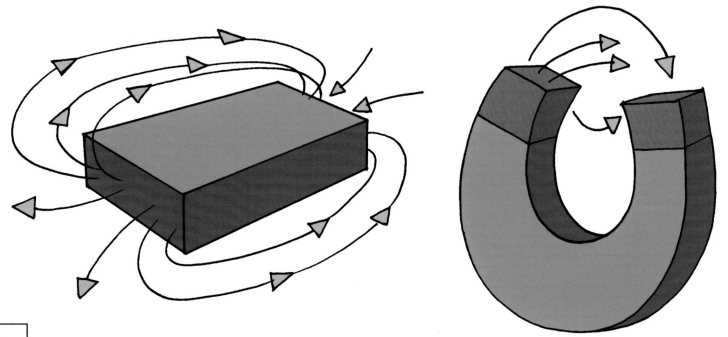

SUPPOSE YOU HAD DISCOVERED THE MAGNETIC OR ELECTRIC FIELDS OF FORCE. WHAT WOULD YOU DO? MY GUESS IS YOU'D DO WHAT THE FIRST DISCOVERERS DID. YOU'D PLAY WITH THEM, OF COURSE. GUESS WHAT? YOU STILL CAN! THIS BOOK SHOWS YOU HOW.

2 MEET THE MAGNET

A magnet is one of the greatest toys in the world. You can let your imagination go wild when you play with one. You can get a bar magnet or a horseshoe magnet at most toy stores. Here are some things you can do:

- Go on a hunt for magnetic attraction.

> **BE A DETECTIVE. MAKE DISCOVERIES AS YOU WALK AROUND YOUR HOUSE. TAKE A MAGNET AND DISCOVER ALL THE THINGS IT ATTRACTS. DO NOT PUT YOUR MAGNET ON A COMPUTER OR AN AUDIOTAPE OR EVEN A CD. THEY WILL BE RUINED. HERE'S A LIST TO GET YOU STARTED.**

TRY:

forks, knives, spoons	paper	glasses
pots and pans	dishes	the kitchen sink
paper clips	steel wool	bathroom faucets

- Make a paper clip chain. Let one end of a paper clip stick to your magnet. Touch another paper clip to the free end of the first one and keep going. See how long a chain you can make. If you have another magnet, make another paper clip chain. The magnet with the longest chain has the strongest force field.

- Does a magnet's field pass through paper? Put a paper clip on top of a piece of paper with the magnet underneath. Can you move the clip around by moving the magnet? What other materials can the field pass through? Try a plastic container cover, a paper plate, a china dish, or a tabletop.

- Make your invisible magnetic field visible. You will need extra-fine steel wool from the hardware store, scissors, paper, and a magnet. Put the paper over the magnet. Snip and spread tiny pieces of steel wool evenly over the paper. Watch as they move to show the magnetic field around the magnet underneath. The lines of force go from one end of the magnet to the other.

BABY OIL

See your magnetic field in 3-D. Fill a clear plastic bottle with baby oil, salad oil, or clear liquid shampoo. Add about a teaspoon of tiny steel wool pieces. Shake the jar. Put the end of a bar magnet on the side of the bottle. Ta da! You can see the suspended steel particles take the shape of the magnetic field.

- Play with two magnets. Do they attract each other? The answer is, sometimes. Other times they push each other away. Put two magnets near each other and cover them with a piece of paper. Show their fields of force by sprinkling tiny pieces of steel wool on the paper. Use two bar magnets to show the fields when the ends of the magnets attract each other and when they repel each other. The ends of the magnets are their poles. One end of a magnet is called north and the other is called south.

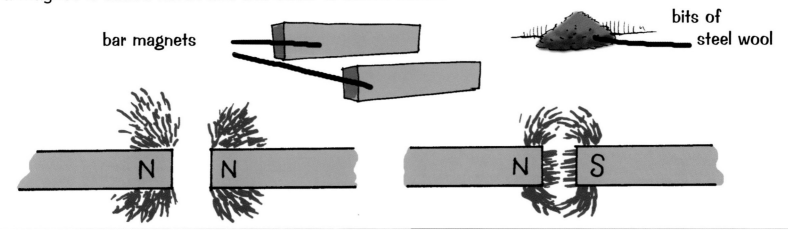

bar magnets

bits of steel wool

N   N   N   S

ACTUALLY ONE END IS REALLY THE NORTH-SEEKING POLE AND THE OTHER THE SOUTH-SEEKING POLE. HANG A BAR MAGNET BY A STRING TIED TO ITS MIDDLE SO THAT IT IS BALANCED. LET THE MAGNET SWING FREELY. IT WILL LINE UP WITH ONE END POINTING NORTH. THE EARTH ACTS LIKE A GIANT MAGNET. ITS FIELD OF FORCE ACTS ON YOUR BAR MAGNET. SO THE NORTH POLE OF YOUR BAR MAGNET IS ATTRACTED TO THE EARTH'S NORTH POLE. I HOPE YOU'RE NOT TOO CONFUSED.

BRAIN CRAMP!

All magnets, no matter what their shape, have two poles. North and south poles attract each other. But two norths repel each other, and two souths repel each other also.

TO SUM IT UP: UNLIKE POLES ATTRACT. LIKE POLES REPEL.

WHENEVER A SCIENTIST MAKES A DISCOVERY, SOONER OR LATER SOMEONE SAYS, "IS THERE ANY WAY I CAN USE THIS IDEA?" HERE ARE SOME THINGS YOU CAN USE A MAGNET FOR.

- Use a magnet to make another magnet. Get a large nail. Make sure it is attracted to a magnet. Stroke the nail at least 20 times in the same direction with one pole of a bar magnet. Does the nail now pick up metal paper clips? Test it and see.

- A magnet comes in handy if you spill a box of pins or nails. Instead of picking them up one by one, a magnet can collect groups of them at one time.

- Collect meteorites on the beach. Rocks from the solar system are constantly raining onto the earth's atmosphere. These space rocks are moving so fast that most of them completely burn up before they can fall to earth. Most of the material that reaches the earth's surface is so tiny you can hardly see it. But you can collect it with a magnet because meteorites are made of iron.

Put a magnet in a plastic bag and tie the bag closed with a string. Now drag it along the sand. The magnet will attract iron dust from outer space on the outside of the bag. To capture the dust, turn the bag inside out as you remove the magnet. Look at your space dust with a magnifying lens. Meteorites are almost perfect little balls.

WHEN THE METEORITES HIT THE ATMOSPHERE, THEY WERE HEATED UNTIL THEY MELTED. THE MELTED METAL, LIKE OTHER LIQUIDS, TAKES THE SHAPE OF A SPHERE AS IT FALLS TO EARTH. RAINDROPS ARE ALSO BALLS, NOT TEAR-DROP SHAPED, WHEN THEY ARE IN MIDAIR.

• Some breakfast cereals, such as Instant Cream of Wheat, contain iron and say so on the box.

I AM *IRONMAN!*

Put some dry Instant Cream of Wheat and a magnet in a plastic bag. Shake the bag. Pull out the magnet and carefully brush the very tiny pieces of iron onto a sheet of white paper. Put the magnet under the paper and move the edible metal around.

Some flake cereals also advertise that they contain iron. But the iron is trapped in the flakes. To get it out, put some dried flakes in a plastic bag and smash them with a rolling pin. Put the smashed flakes into a new plastic bag (with no holes), and add water and a magnet. Shake. Now you should be able to retrieve the iron, which sticks to the magnet.

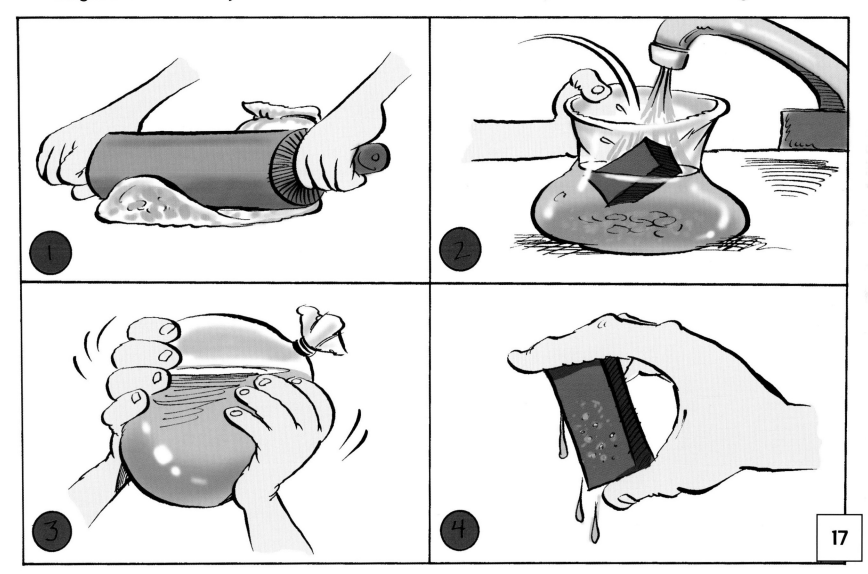

3  HAIR-RAISING SHOCKERS

YOU DON'T HAVE TO BE SCARED TO MAKE YOUR HAIR STAND ON END. IN FACT, THE HAIR ON YOUR ARMS LETS YOU FEEL AN ELECTRIC FIELD. SO ROLL UP YOUR SLEEVE FOR THIS EXPERIMENT.

You can't feel a magnetic field, but you can feel an electric one. On a clear, dry day, rub a blown-up balloon against a wool sweater. Then move the balloon over your arm. Feel the hair on your arm stand on end. Move the balloon over your head. Guess what? Your hair stands up! The balloon is charged with static electricity. The word "static" means "standing still." The electricity isn't going any place.

Touch the balloon to your arm. What happens to the electric field? The field of force disappears. The electricity ran into your arm. But you can recharge it the same way you created it in the first place.

A balloon that has an electric field can do some strange things. Try them out. Stick a charged balloon on a wall. It stays where you put it! Move a charged balloon over some dried cereal, such as Puffed Rice. You can make the cereal dance! If it gets too close, some of the cereal will leap up and attach itself to the balloon.

YOU CAN ALWAYS MAKE THE FIELD DISAPPEAR BY TOUCHING THE CHARGED AREA WITH YOUR HAND, TO SOME OTHER OBJECT, OR TO THE GROUND. WHEN YOU GIVE A CHARGE A WAY TO DISAPPEAR, YOU ARE "GROUNDING" IT. ON A RAINY DAY, THE CHARGE "LEAKS" AWAY TO MOISTURE IN THE AIR. BUT IF THE DAY IS CRISP AND DRY, YOU MAY HAVE A HARD TIME GROUNDING YOUR BALLOON. RUB IT WITH A FABRIC-SOFTENER SHEET. THE ANTI-STATIC INGREDIENTS IN THE SHEET DO THE JOB!

Here are some other ways you can create electric fields:

• See an electric "wind" with Scotch Magic™ Tape. Pull off a piece of tape about 6 inches long (15 centimeters). Bring the tape close to a charged balloon. Does the tape move toward the balloon or away from it? Stick the tape to a Formica™ countertop, leaving an end free. Quickly pull the tape off the countertop to charge it. Bring the tape near the balloon. What happens?

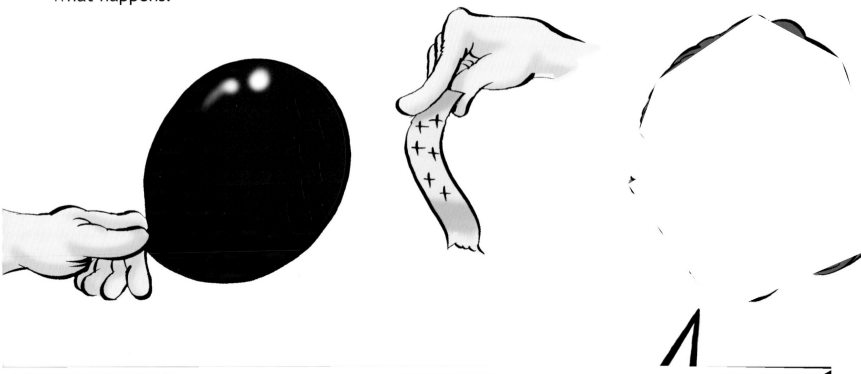

ARE YOU GETTING THE IDEA THAT THERE MAY BE TWO KINDS OF ELECTRIC FIELDS, JUST AS THERE ARE TWO POLES WITH A MAGNETIC FIELD? KEEP ON EXPERIMENTING.

• On a clear, dry day, rub a nylon stocking or panty-hose with a wool sweater. As the stocking becomes charged, the sides repel each other. The stocking becomes three dimensional.

HOW CAN THIS BE? THINK ABOUT THIS. THE ENTIRE STOCKING IS GETTING THE SAME KIND OF ELECTRICITY. THE STOCKING TAKES A SHAPE AS THE OPPOSITE SIDES OF IT REPEL EACH OTHER. JUST AS SIMILAR POLES REPEL EACH OTHER IN MAGNETISM, SIMILAR ELECTRIC CHARGES REPEL EACH OTHER.

• What happens if you rub nylon with a balloon? The nylon and the balloon stick to each other, that's what! Now you've discovered that opposite charges attract each other.

You'll get a charge out of this. There are two kinds of electricity. We call them positive and negative. Scientists have figured out which materials become positive and which become negative when they come into contact with each other. You can experiment by rubbing opposites together. Here's the list with the most positive at the top, to the most negative.

rabbit fur   (+) most positive
glass
human hair
nylon
wool
fur
silk
paper
                    zero
wood
amber
sealing wax
hard rubber
rayon
polyester
Saran Wrap™
rubber balloon
Teflon™   (–) most negative

Help! I Can't Get Rid Of This Balloon!

If you rub two items that are next to each other on the list, you can still create an electric field. The item that is closer to "most positive" will become positively charged, and the item that is closer to "most negative" will become negatively charged.

When you comb your hair with a hard rubber comb, your hair becomes positively charged and the comb becomes negatively charged. If you pull apart nylon and polyester garments from the dryer, the nylon item will be positive, and the polyester will be negative.

IF YOU WANT TO SEE SPARKS FLY, DON'T USE FABRIC SOFTENER IN THE DRYER AND EMPTY THE DRYER IN THE DARK. THE TINY FLASHES OF LIGHT ARE LIKE MINIATURE LIGHTNING BOLTS.

4 MAKE AN ELECTRIC FIELD DETECTOR

AFTER SCIENTISTS ANNOUNCE A DISCOVERY, PEOPLE SCRATCH THEIR HEADS AND WONDER WHAT TO DO WITH IT. IF THE DISCOVERY IS USED TO MAKE AN INVENTION, IT'S CALLED TECHNOLOGY. USE THE DISCOVERY THAT SCOTCH MAGIC™ TAPE CAN BE ELECTRICALLY CHARGED TO BUILD AN INSTRUMENT THAT CAN DETECT THE CHARGES OTHER THINGS HAVE.

Your electric field detector is called an electroscope. To build one, you will need: a flexible plastic drinking straw
an empty film can
a sharp pencil
Scotch Magic™ Tape

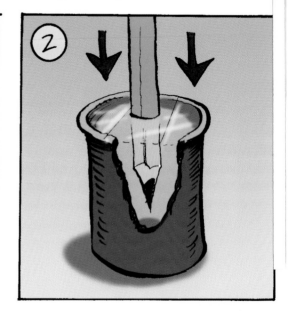

1. Cover the open end of a film can with a few pieces of tape.
2. Poke a hole in the tape with the point of a sharp pencil. This will be your electroscope base.
3. Bend the straw into an "L" shape.
4. Stick the longer end of the "L" into the hole in the tape.
5. Now for the important part of the electroscope. Tear off a piece of tape about 4 inches long (10 centimeters). Stick it on a Formica™ countertop, leaving a tab. Use the tab to quickly pull the tape off the counter. The tape now has a negative charge. Lay the center of the tape sticky side up across the bent-over straw.

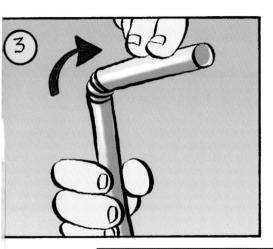
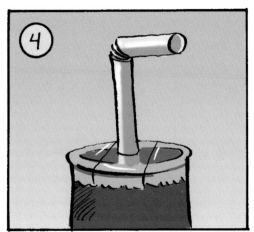

NOTICE HOW THE TWO ENDS OF THE TAPE SEPARATE. THEY REPEL EACH OTHER BECAUSE THEY HAVE THE SAME CHARGE.

Bring a few of the charged objects from the last experiment near the electroscope. If the tape moves toward the object, the object has a positive charge. If it moves away, the charge is negative. After a while, you will have to recharge the tape by pressing it on the counter and ripping it off again.

5  A CHARGE GOES AND FLOWS

Here's a shocking fact: When you rub your feet against a rug as you walk across a room and then bring your finger near a metal doorknob, you get—"Ouch!"—shocked!

YOU BECOME A CHARGED OBJECT. THE ELECTRICITY IS MORE ATTRACTED TO A DOORKNOB THAN IT IS TO YOU. IT CRACKLES THROUGH THE AIR AS IT "GROUNDS" ITSELF ON THE DOORKNOB. YOU GET A LITTLE SHOCK. LIGHTNING IS A VERY BIG VERSION OF THIS.

Metals strongly attract electricity. And electricity behaves very differently in metals than it does in nonmetals. Electricity in nonmetals is static—it doesn't go anywhere. But electricity in metals moves. If the metal is a wire, electricity flows through the wire in an electric current.

WHAT A DISCOVERY AN ELECTRIC CURRENT WAS! TECHNOLOGY TOOK A GIANT LEAP FORWARD. THINK OF ALL THE INVENTIONS THAT WORK BECAUSE OF ELECTRICITY. BUT WE'RE GETTING AHEAD OF OUR STORY.

An object that is charged with static electricity is not a steady source of electrical current. When it is grounded, the charge quickly disappears. Wouldn't it be nice if we could store up electricity so that we could get it when we want it? Guess what? We can! Electricity is stored in batteries.

You can make a battery with your tongue. You will need a piece of aluminum foil and something silver, such as a piece of jewelry or a silver fork. Taste the aluminum foil. Now taste the silver. Nothing happens. Touch the foil and the silver. Put your tongue at the place where the silver and aluminum foil meet. You'll feel a tingling. Electricity flows in a circle from one metal to the other through the saliva on your tongue and back to the metals. The key to a battery is very simple—you need two different metals and a liquid called an electrolyte that conducts electricity. Saliva is a very weak electrolyte. Acids and salt water are also electrolytes.

And I Thought They Had Me Doing Weird Stuff In These Books!

The word "battery" means a number of small things used together as a single unit. The first electric battery ever invented was made from pairs of two different metals layered like a sandwich. In between each pair of metals was a blotter soaked with salt water.

The first batteries were large and wet, and not very portable. Modern batteries are small and can provide electricity anywhere you might want it. They are also dry, and some can be recharged after the electricity is used up.

A battery sends an electric current through a wire. But in order to get the current to flow, both ends of the wire must connect to the battery. A closed circle of electricity is called an electric circuit.

See for yourself. You can buy your supplies at a hardware or electronics store. You will need:

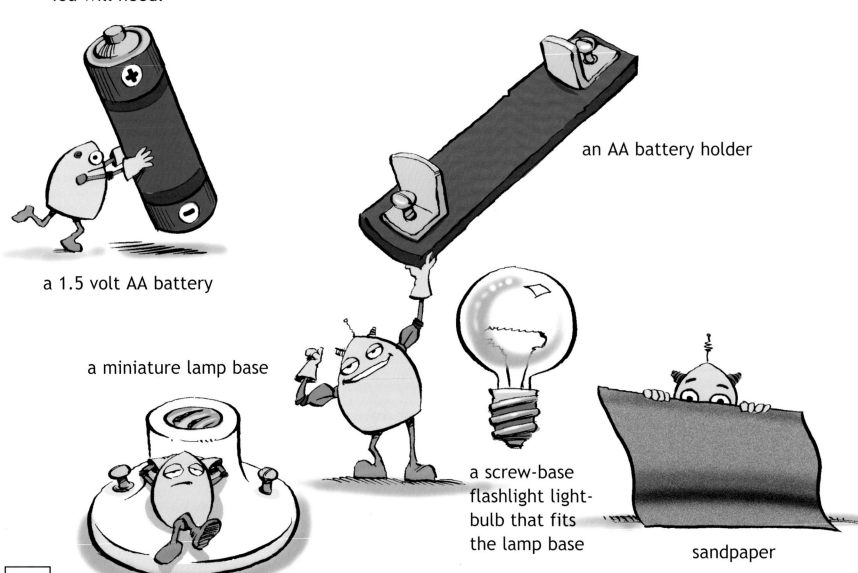

an AA battery holder

a 1.5 volt AA battery

a miniature lamp base

a screw-base flashlight light-bulb that fits the lamp base

sandpaper

A battery holder has metal contacts for each end of a battery, with wires called leads (feeds) coming from each contact. Put the battery in the battery holder, making sure to match the positive and negative ends of the battery with the contacts in the battery holder. Screw the bulb into the lamp base. Attach one of the lead wires into the hole of one of the metal eyelets of the lamp base.

YOU MAY NEED TO EXPOSE A LONGER PIECE OF EACH WIRE LEAD. TO STRIP THE WIRE OF INSULATION, GENTLY CUT THROUGH ONLY THE INSULATION WITH A SCISSORS. FOLD A PIECE OF SANDPAPER AROUND THE CUT END. PULL ON THE INSULATION WITH THE SANDPAPER. IT SHOULD COME RIGHT OFF, LEAVING BARE WIRE BEHIND.

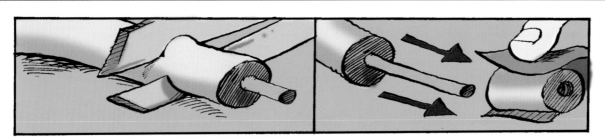

Touch the stripped end of the other lead wire to the other lamp-base eyelet. What happens?

Congratulations! You've just completed an electric circuit. The instant you connect the wire, electricity flows from the battery through the wire, through the bulb (which lights up), and back through the wire to the battery. When you disconnect a wire, the circuit is broken and the electric current no longer flows.

A SWITCH IS A DEVICE THAT COMPLETES OR BREAKS A CIRCUIT SO YOU DON'T HAVE TO TOUCH THE WIRES DIRECTLY. THE SIMPLE IDEA OF A CIRCUIT IS USED FOR ALL KINDS OF INVENTIONS. ELECTRICAL ENGINEERS FIGURE OUT HOW TO MAKE THINGS WORK BY USING ELECTRIC CIRCUITS.

 # THE FIELD FROM FLOWING ELECTRICITY

ELECTRIC CURRENT AND ELECTRIC CIRCUITS ARE GREAT DISCOVERIES THAT HAVE LED TO VERY USEFUL INVENTIONS. BUT THIS BOOK IS ABOUT SOURCES OF FORCES. YOU MIGHT THINK WE'VE GOTTEN AWAY FROM OUR STORY. NOT SO! WHEREVER THERE IS AN ELECTRIC CURRENT, THERE'S ALSO A FIELD OF FORCE.

Is there a connection between magnetism and electricity? How can you detect a field of force around a wire? A simple experiment answers both questions at once. All you need is your homemade electric circuit from the last experiment and a compass.

Turn the compass so that the needle lines up with north. Complete your circuit so the bulb lights. Move one of the wires near the compass needle. The needle will move slightly. There it is! Proof that a field of force surrounds the wire. The field is strong enough to deflect the compass needle. The needle moves only when the circuit is complete and electricity is flowing through the wire.

You will need:

a spool (about 25 feet [8 meters]) of lightweight insulated hook-up wire (from a hardware or electronics store)

a compass

tape (any kind will do)

Real Men Use Duct Tape!

sandpaper

a soda can

The field of force around a wire carrying a current is very weak. How can you make it stronger? The obvious way is to add more wire. How can you do that? By making a coil. Wrap about 30 turns of the wire around a soda can. Leave about 3 inches (8 centimeters) of bare wire on both leads. Use scissors and sandpaper as directed in the last experiment to strip the insulation off the two ends. Remove the coil of wire from the can, and tape it together in two places. Tape the coil vertically on a table in a north-south direction. Place the compass inside the coil so that the needle is pointing north. The wires of the coil and the needle will line up in the same direction.

CONGRATULATIONS! YOU'VE JUST BUILT A GALVANOMETER. THE COMPASS NEEDLE IS A PERMANENT MAGNET. THE FIELD OF FORCE AROUND A WIRE CARRYING AN ELECTRIC CURRENT ACTS LIKE A MAGNET AND MAKES THE COMPASS NEEDLE MOVE.

Test the battery in the battery holder. Connect one battery holder lead to a lead from the coil by twisting them together. Touch the other battery lead to the other coil lead. What happens to the compass needle?

You can test other batteries in your house. You don't need to have them in battery holders. Just touch the leads from the coil to the top and bottom of a battery. If the compass needle doesn't move, you've got a dead battery.

7  AN ELECTROMAGNET

BY NOW YOU'RE PROBABLY GETTING A GOOD IDEA ABOUT HOW SCIENCE WORKS. THE GALVANOMETER SHOWS A PERMANENT MAGNET (THE COMPASS NEEDLE) REACTING TO THE FIELD OF FORCE AROUND AN ELECTRIC CURRENT (THE WIRE). ARE YOU READY FOR THE NEXT LOGICAL QUESTION?

Do you think an electric current can be used to create a magnet?
You bet! Here's what you need to make an electric magnet or "electromagnet."

AA battery in its battery holder
an iron nail at least 2$\frac{1}{2}$ inches (6 centimeters) long
hook-up wire
paper clips

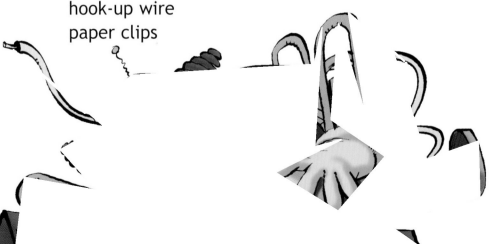

Starting at the nail head and leaving a 2-inch (5 centimeters) lead, wind the wire neatly around the nail. When you are almost to the tip, wind a second layer back on top of the first.

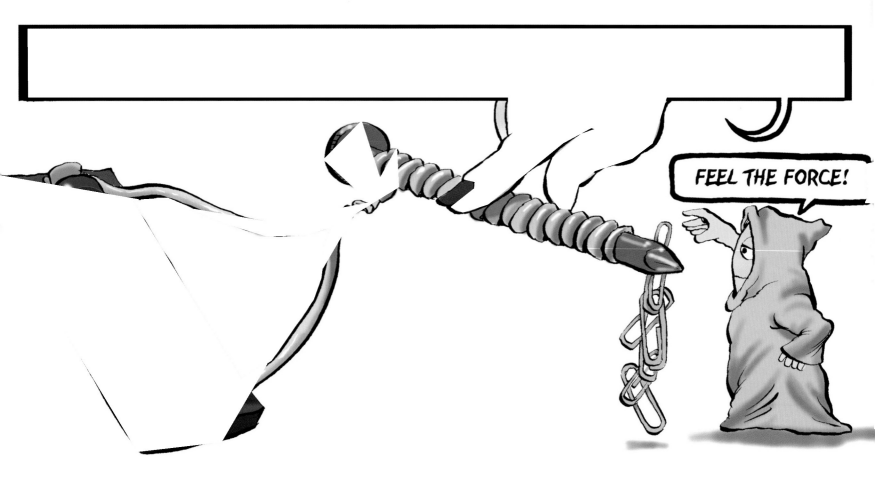

FEEL THE FORCE!

Leave a second lead of about 2 inches (5 centimeters). Twist the two leads together to keep the coil tight. Strip $1/2$ inch (1.3 centimeters) of the insulation from the ends of both leads. Connect one lead from the nail to a lead from the battery holder. As you complete the circuit by connecting the remaining leads, touch the nail to a paper clip. When the circuit is complete, the nail becomes an electromagnet. Make a paper clip chain with your new electromagnet! When the circuit is broken, the electromagnet no longer can lift the paper clips.

ELECTROMAGNETS CAN LIFT VERY HEAVY LOADS, AS LONG AS THE LOADS ARE MADE OF IRON OR STEEL. THEY ARE USED IN AUTOMOBILE JUNKYARDS AND STEEL MILLS.

EVERY ONCE IN A WHILE A SCIENTIST ASKS A QUESTION THAT LEADS TO A DISCOVERY THAT CHANGES THE WORLD. HERE'S ONE OF THOSE QUESTIONS: IF ELECTRIC CURRENT CAN CREATE A MAGNET, CAN A MAGNET BE USED TO CREATE ELECTRICITY?

In the early part of the nineteenth century, a young English chemist and physicist named Michael Faraday asked this question. He removed the metal core from an electromagnet and attached the ends of the wire coil to a galvanometer. When he moved a bar magnet back and forth through the coil, the needle on the galvanometer moved for an instant. The moving magnetic field had produced a momentary electric current. Faraday noticed that he got a current only when the wires were at right angles to the moving magnetic field.

Faraday figured that if he could somehow keep the magnet moving, he could generate large amounts of electricity. In 1831, he invented the first electric generator. Instead of moving the magnet, he spun a copper disk that cut through the magnet's field of force. Wires attached the disk to a galvanometer. A continuous flow of electricity came from Faraday's "dynamo."

Modern power plants generate enormous amounts of electricity. They use huge magnets and thousands of coils of wires. They keep the magnets moving by using something like a pinwheel, called a turbine. Turbines can be moved by falling water, or by steam, or by wind. The first power plants were built about 50 years after Faraday's incredible discovery.

IN ADDITION TO INVENTING THE GENERATOR, MICHAEL FARADAY WAS THE FIRST PERSON TO USE THE TERMS "FIELDS OF FORCE" AND "ELECTROLYTES." HE CAME FROM A POOR FAMILY AND HAD NINE BROTHERS AND SISTERS. HE NEVER FINISHED SCHOOL. WHEN HE WAS THIRTEEN, HE WENT TO WORK FOR A BOOKBINDER. HE READ LOTS OF BOOKS AND DISCOVERED HIS LOVE FOR SCIENCE. MICHAEL FARADAY IS AN EXAMPLE OF A PERSON WHO EDUCATED HIMSELF. PRETTY AMAZING!

9  THE FORCE THAT'S ALWAYS WITH US

You live in a field of force. Let go of an object and it falls. It is attracted to the Earth. The field of force is none other than gravity. Gravity is the force of attraction between two bodies of matter. It is a very weak force, much weaker than electrical or magnetic forces. It is easily measured only when we are dealing with a great deal of matter, like the planet Earth. Your weight is a measurement of how much the Earth attracts you.

SINCE YOUR BODY IS MADE OF MATTER, IT IS REASONABLE TO THINK THAT YOUR GRAVITY CAN ATTRACT OTHER MATTER. BUT YOU ARE MADE OF SUCH A SMALL AMOUNT OF MATTER THAT YOUR FIELD OF GRAVITATIONAL FORCE IS IMPOSSIBLE TO NOTICE.

A gravitational field is like electrical and magnetic fields. All of them pull objects that are in their force fields. One big difference is that gravity only attracts. It doesn't repel. The Earth's gravity attracts the moon. The moon's gravity attracts the water on the surface of the Earth and causes tides. The sun's gravity attracts the Earth. Electrical and magnetic forces repel as well as attract.

What causes these fields of force? We have a pretty good idea of what causes electrical and magnetic fields. This idea is called a theory.

SCIENTISTS DREAM UP THEORIES TO EXPLAIN LOTS OF DISCOVERIES. THEORIES CAN BE USEFUL BECAUSE THEY OFTEN SUGGEST EXPERIMENTS. BUT THEORIES ARE NOT CARVED IN STONE. SOMETIMES THERE WILL BE A DISCOVERY THAT DOESN'T FIT WITH A THEORY. THEN THE THEORY HAS TO BE CHANGED.

Here's a brief look at the theory that explains electricity and magnetism:

THIS IS A VERY COMPLICATED THEORY, SO WE WANT TO JUST GIVE YOU A NUTSHELL VERSION.

protons

nucleus

electrons

All matter is made of extremely small particles called atoms. In every atom there are even smaller particles that have both positive and negative electrical charges. The negative particles are called electrons. The positive particles are in the center of the atom, called the nucleus. In most atoms, the numbers of positive and negative electrical charges are equal. When the charges are balanced, the matter has no electrical charge.

Electrons are like tiny planets orbiting the nucleus. In iron, the electron orbits of most atoms are lined up in the same direction. This is what makes a magnet a magnet. In most materials, the electron orbits are in random directions. They are not magnetic.

In static electricity between a comb and your hair, electrons leave one material and go to the other. The comb gets extra electrons, so it becomes negatively charged. Your hair has lost electrons, leaving it positively charged. When an object with static electricity is grounded, it gets rid of or picks up electrons to restore a balance.

COMB

HAIR

An electric current is the flow of electrons through a wire. Electrons move from atom to atom. Metals lose electrons easily, so they are good electrical conductors. Nonmetals don't lose electrons easily, so they are good insulators. The materials that become charged with static electricity are mostly insulators, not conductors.

THE OVERALL ELECTRICAL CHARGE ON THE EARTH AND THE MOON IS ZERO. ALL THE POSITIVES AND NEGATIVES CANCEL EACH OTHER OUT. THAT'S WHY THE ONLY FIELD OF FORCE AT WORK IN SPACE IS GRAVITY. BUT THE IRON CORE AT THE CENTER OF THE EARTH GIVES IT A MAGNETIC FIELD. ALTHOUGH WE DO HAVE SOME UNDERSTANDING OF WHAT CAUSES ELECTRICITY AND MAGNETISM, THE CAUSE OF GRAVITY IS STILL A MYSTERY.

Albert Einstein, one of the greatest scientists of the twentieth century, believed that gravity, electricity, and magnetism could all be explained by a single theory. He called it the "Unified Field Theory." So far no one has found the evidence or the explanation for this theory. There is still much to be discovered. It is waiting for you.